Romans

a daily saturation study
Book 1

Romans

a daily saturation study
Book 1

Jeremiah Bolich

Romans: A Daily Saturation Study (book 1)
© 2017 by Jeremiah Bolich

ISBN-10: 0998726508
ISBN-13: 9780998726502

Cross Style Press
Lebanon, Tennessee

Published in the United States of America.

JeremiahBolich.com

Introduction

It was probably from Corinth, sometime in the year AD 56, where Tertius (16:22) penned Paul's dictation to the Church in Rome. It is apparent from the letter (15:23-24) that Paul planned to visit the believers in Rome on his way to Spain from Jerusalem on what would be his last missionary journey. Paul's desire to visit their ministry, which he did not begin, was coupled with his longing to encourage the believers in Rome and to have them assist him in his journey.

Paul's letter to the church in Rome served as not only an announcement of his coming, but also a reminder to the church of their position in the Kingdom of God. It is not only the Jew who benefits from God's promise to Abraham, but the Gentile also (1:16, 30). Paul's statement in 1:17, "For in the gospel a righteousness from God is revealed, a righteousness that is by faith from first to last, just as it is written: 'The righteous will live by faith,'" serves to underline the thrust of his message. In this Bible Saturation series, we will walk through Paul's address to the believers in Rome and discover, verse by verse, the life-changing truth of his message.

• • • • •

This book is a series in Biblical Saturation. Saturation is the process of the Living Word [Jesus] revealing Himself through the Written Word [the Bible]. As collected and recorded through various writers, the Bible is the revelation of God through the second person of the Godhead, Jesus the Christ.

Our attempt in this study is to engage with Jesus Christ through His Word. He alone reveals the Truth of Scripture. Although Saturation Bible Study includes times of study and research, Jesus often reveals the Truth of a particular passage in the normal routines of life. This launches our Bible Study times from an enclosed and removed setting into the everyday routines of life. Our engagement with Jesus through His Word is better described as a lifestyle than a study habit. Saturation is not so much about studying a book, as it is walking in intimacy with a person.

Saturation Bible Study is all about saturating in the presence of Jesus through His Word. While saturating in His Word, walking and talking with Jesus through your day, you will find Jesus revealing Himself to your through the passage you as studying. Jesus wants to speak to you. He wants to reveal Himself to you. The Bible is the avenue that clarifies absolutely who Jesus is and what He is communicating—and Jesus does not speak contrary to His Word.

Slave
Romans 1:1

Titles. Titles give us information about people. Over the years, I've had many of them. I've been called neighbor, student, pastor, waiter, boss, and many others. These titles give people a reference point for understanding me. In every walk of life, titles are used in this way.

In Paul's opening statement to the church in Rome, he uses a few different titles. The first among these is the title **servant**. The word **servant** comes from the Greek Word **doulos**, which can be translated either servant or slave. This word is used over 200 times in our NT and is consistently used to describes a Christian.

Slave is a graphic title to attach to anyone. Is it really accurate to apply it to Christians? Paul would emphatically say, "Yes!" As believers, we have surrendered our lives to Christ, our Master. We've given up freedoms, rights, comforts, and pleasures. We take His Word over our own, His desires over our desires, and His plan over our plans. He is the Master, we are his servants. As Paul will claim later (Rom 6:22), we were created to be "slaves to God." We were created to be slaves to Christ!

Although slavery is graphic imagery, it fits well with most of the language Jesus used in His teaching. Extreme and Jesus more often than not go hand in hand. After all, we have still today the symbol of Roman capital punishment as the center of our Christian faith. Jesus commanded, take up your cross and follow me. There was no trickery in Jesus' call, we all know full well the cost Christianity brings.

This is the language Paul used to introduce himself to the church in Rome, then throughout his letter, to refer to those who embrace Jesus as their savior. From the beginning to the end, we are called to be slaves for Christ.

REFLECTION

1. Do you see yourself as a slave of Christ?

2. If you were to put this call of Christ in your own words, how would you describe Christianity to a friend or coworker?

3. What area of your heart is not surrendered to Jesus?

Apostle
Romans 1:1

In Paul's opening statement to the church in Rome, he uses a few different titles to describe himself. We've taken a closer look at **servant**. Let's now consider **Apostle**.

This word is a translation of the Greek word **apostolos**. We generally define this word as **one sent** or **ambassador**, however this word also represents in Christianity the specific group of people who were first sent by Christ. They were eye-witnesses of His earthly ministry. They were the Apostles, those who were sent by Jesus Himself.

Normally this would exclude the vast majority (all but the original 12 disciples plus Paul) of those who call or have called themselves Christian. Yet as we look through the NT, we find others who have received the call of **apostello**.

So, how does this work? What's the difference between the first Apostles and those of us who have also been sent as they were?

The Apostles are unique, for they were the first, but their Apostleship was to serve as an example to us. They are what every Christian is supposed to look like. They are the example. They were the first curriers of the Truth. As they are sent, you and I are also. Their mission, passion, and dedication was to continue in our life. We only make a distinction between them and the rest of Christ's Church because they were sent first.

Often times, preachers pour over dictionaries and original language tools to discover the meaning of such words. These are always helpful and I myself use many of these. Yet sometimes, as is the example here, living examples serve better than books. For the church in Rome, Paul was their example. He demonstrated "being sent."

It makes me wonder…Who are we an example to? Are we demonstrating to a lost world what the Christian life is supposed to look like? Are we accurately demonstrating what it means to "be sent" by Christ?

REFLECTION

1. Would you describe yourself as a good example for others to follow?

2. Do you see yourself as an apostle? If so, to whom has God sent you? Your family? Your friends? Explain.

Set Apart
Romans 1:1

We've covered two of the three titles Paul uses in his introduction to the church in Rome. The last title he uses is **set apart**. Paul proclaims that he is set apart "for the gospel of God."

The Greek word we translate **set apart** means just what you think it means. It means to be set apart. I set apart some of my income for date nights with my wife, Karenda. I set apart a portion of my day to spend solely with my kids. To set apart something is to reserve it for something entirely.

To apply this word in such an absolute, life-encompassing way seems rather extreme, yet for Paul, this is the simplest definition for Christianity. The Christian is **set apart** completely for the Good News of Jesus Christ. The Christian is **set apart** in their thought-life, schedules, routines, responses, reactions, dreams for the future — every area of life. This is Paul, but it is also supposed to be you and me.

I had a conversation about being **set apart** with one of my closest friends a few years ago. He is now in full-time evangelism and travels with his wife and daughter, but at the time of our conversation, he was a computer programer for a software company. He used to complain to me how, in his particular job, it was impossible for him to saturate in the Word while trying to focus on programming. Looking back on that conversation, I was trying to describe to him what it means to be *set-apart*.

Being **set apart** to Christ is not a removal of your normal routines or responsibilities, rather it is an invitation for Jesus to join you in those activities. Jesus knows your life, your routines — He created you and foresaw you in your current lifestyle. He does not want to interrupt your day, He wants to join you throughout your day.

REFLECTION

1. Take a few minutes and think over your life. Your job, fun-times, relaxing-times, and every other area of your life. Are you set apart for Him in all those areas? Why or why not?

2. In what areas of your life are you not completely His, not completely set apart?

3. How might Romans 1:1 change your life from this point forward?

It's All About Jesus
Romans 1:2-4

Paul tells us that the Gospel, which means the **Good News**, finally came in the arrival of Jesus. He is the Good News! Jesus is what God had promised, what He was so excited about! When the angels came to the shepherds in the field, they rejoiced over the arrival of Jesus. They proclaimed, "Fear not! …behold, I bring you good tidings of great joy…" (Luke 2:10 KJV)

In light of all that God did throughout the OT, His focus was to prepare us for the coming of His Son. God's aim wasn't to establish traditions, routines, or laws. These were steps on a staircase which were to lead us to Jesus. The goal of a staircase is to lead us to the top, the journey's end. Jesus is the final stop in God's plan to redeem us.

Christianity is about Jesus. Paul begins his letter reminding the church in Rome of this fact. Jesus is the Good News, the living example to all mankind of what mankind should look like. As He lived, I also live. As He was set apart, a slave to God, I am to be also. And this is only possible by walking with Him every moment of every day. I am His and He is mine.

REFLECTION

1. Does this describe your life with Jesus?

2. Like me, you've probably seen other versions of Christianity lived-out in our modern religious culture. How does Romans 1:2-4 challenge the way Christianity is often described?

3. Do you know anyone who thinks their religious, yet doesn't seem to walk in a personal relationship with Jesus? How should you talk with that person? How could you remind them that Christianity is all about Jesus?

The Divinity of Jesus
Romans 1:3

Continuing into verse 3, we find Paul gives us some valuable insight into Jesus. This will take several days to walk through, to wrap our mind around what Paul is presenting. Let's begin by looking at the divinity of Jesus.

If you've spent anytime around Church, you've probably heard that Jesus is God. This is absolutely true. Though Jesus was born into humanity, He has always been. He was not created, but existed with God "in the beginning." (John 1:1-2) In John's Gospel, he reminds his readers of Genesis 1:1 — "In the beginning..." Jesus' existence reached back to this time of our beginning.

John, like Paul, tries to show how God was present when humanity first began. The "In the beginning..." of Genesis 1:1 is not a record of God's beginning, but our beginning. When Adam first came onto the scene, God was already there. God had always been there. God is that from which everything finds its beginning.

This is the starting point for Paul whenever he describes Jesus. Jesus was not merely a man, He was the God-man. Jesus was God who became a man, lived as a man, and died as a man. Thus, God became one of us. Jesus, the divine Son of God, became a man.

REFLECTION

1. Why is this important? Why does Paul bring this up to the church in Rome?

2. Christianity is not centered around man's love for man. Christianity is centered around God's love for man. Remember, it is "For God so loved the world…" (John 3:16) that we have hope. It is because God loves us and initiated our redemption that we can be saved. The Good News of Christianity is that God, our creator, loves us and has come to save us.

3. I wonder what would happen if we realized God acts on our behalf out of love? God does not want to enslave us. God does not want to control us. God acts in our life always for our benefit. He loves us. If we were to stubbornly cling to this Truth, do you think we might respond to His leading and directing in our life more often? I wonder, would we not ignore Him, put Him off, or rationalize away His promptings in our life?

The Humanity of Jesus
Romans 1:3

As we continue to focus on Paul's description of Jesus in verse 3, we want to remember that his starting point in describing Jesus is that He is God. Jesus wasn't just a man, He was God who came down and took on flesh. God became one of us, God become a man.

So, what does that mean for us…

Whenever we speak of Jesus as the God-man, questions arise. Questions like, what kind of man was He? Was He like LeBron James or like me? Was He beautiful or average looking? Was He a super-man or a normal-man?

Take a few minutes and read Isaiah 53:2-3.

God foretells through the prophet Isaiah what kind of man Jesus would be. Isaiah writes that "he had no beauty or majesty to attract us to Him." There was "nothing in His appearance that we should desire Him." Apparently, Jesus was not a superstar or Hollywood heartthrob. He was born in a poor family, in a poor town, making his living in an unremarkable trade. He was normal, one of us.

I have always marveled at how far Jesus stooped in order to identify with mankind. Although He has come to identify with me, He is unlike me. If I would have had to leave the comforts of being a One-of-a-kind God, I would at least reserve for myself the right to become a one-of-a-kind man. I would have come as a super-man! But He didn't…

Jesus came and assumed all the troubles that we as humans face. He had pesky emotions, unpredictable bodily drives, and a body that worked less and less efficient with every passing year. Jesus came not as the best among us, but in many ways, as the least.

REFLECTION

1. How does this passage change your view of Jesus?

2. What does it mean to you, that Jesus was born an ordinary man?

3. How might Jesus overcoming as an ordinary man encourage you?

4. How might Jesus overcoming as an ordinary man take away excuses for upright living?

Human Nature
Romans 1:3

We are continuing to think-through Paul's description of Jesus in verse 3. Paul describes Jesus as having a human nature. Just as we have a human nature, Jesus also had a human nature.

What is human nature?

Often times, human nature is associated with rebellion against God. This is slightly off the mark. Human nature and rebellion against God, though akin, are not the same thing. Mankind's rebellion against God (Sin) left man to live life independent from God. Thus, in independence from God, man turned to his own emotions and bodily drives as the compass for what is needed to exist in this life. Instead of being sourced by God and being guided by Him, man turned to his own natural drives, his own understandings and his own human nature as his guide in this life.

Paul's description of Jesus in verse 3 reveals that Jesus, like every other human being, had a human nature. Jesus had a body with drives, emotions, cravings, etc. Jesus was a human being with a human nature.

This brings us to some important conclusions about Jesus. First, as Isaiah points out, Jesus was not super-man, He was a normal-man. Secondly, He had the same kind of humanity, the same kind of body that I was born with. Fingers, toes, hair, emotions, and feelings — Jesus had it all. Just as I can experience happiness, fear, and pain, Jesus also could experience these. The five senses I have — see, touch, hear, smell and taste — He also had. Jesus was a human being, just like me.

REFLECTION

1. Do you think God becoming human helps Jesus identify with me? How does a human Jesus help me?

2. If Jesus had a body, just like me, and yet lived a life pleasing to God, shouldn't that show Christians that we too can live a life pleasing to God? Explain.

3. Do you think Jesus had a sex drive?

Sinful Nature
Romans 1:3

The phrase **human nature** is a translation from the Greek word **sarx**. It's more literal translated **flesh.** Paul seems to use the term in this letter to highlight the fallen physical body of mankind. As in Romans 7:18, where the NIV translates sarx **sinful nature**, Paul uses the term to highlight mankind's fallen bodily drives and physical capacity.

Let's continue working through Paul's description of Jesus in verse 3. Paul uses language in his opening statement to the church in Rome to draw their attention to how Jesus became one of us. Just as we have flesh and blood, so does He. What is more, the kind of body Jesus had, every aspect of it, we also have.

When Paul uses the same word (sarx) to describe both Jesus' body and our body, he puts us both on even ground. In other words, Jesus wasn't born in a perfect body, but the same sin-scarred body that we were born with. Our bodies are week and prone to falling apart. We age, get sick, and eventually die. This is human nature and we all experience it. Jesus was born in a body just like ours. He aged, grew tired, and obviously got sick. He was a human being, just like us.

I find it encouraging that no one ever questioned Jesus' humanity. They didn't suspect Him an angel or someone more-than-human. Jesus was a normal, run-of-the-mill human being, just like you and me.

In fact, you might argue, people viewed Jesus as too ordinary. Quite often, Jesus was doubted. When he claimed to be the Messiah, many didn't support Him. Why? Because He was normal — too normal? The Messiah would be super-human, wouldn't He?

It should encourage you that Jesus identified with us in embracing a sin-scarred body. He overcame, for sure. Yet astonishingly, He did it without any physical advantage. The same Spirit by which He overcome, we received from the Father.

REFLECTION

1. Do you think we sometimes grant Jesus a superhero status? Why or why not?

2. What are the dangers of viewing Jesus like a super-hero?

3. If Jesus was super-human, does that change his message?

No Super Hero
Romans 1:3

Does it encourage you that Jesus did not have an advantage over you? I mean, the life He demonstrated to us, one that He calls us to live ourselves, was not demonstrated by one who was super-man. Jesus didn't have an advantage over any other human being.

When I was a kid and would leave the front door open, my mom would yell, "Were you born in a barn?!" If you don't get it, don't fret, it's an Indiana saying. I chuckle now, however, thinking I should have said, "No, but Jesus was!"

Think about it, Jesus was born in a barn. He was not remarkable. He was not beautiful or desirable, but as Isaiah foresaw, "one familiar with suffering." Consider what that means. I wonder...Was Jesus picked on? Was he unpopular? Was he clumsy? What was Jesus really like?

If you've ever been an outcast, one who has failed, been overlooked, fallen short, or pushed aside, then you can probably understand the Biblical Jesus. Jesus was not born as the best of human-kind, but ranked closer to the bottom of the heap.

Be encouraged! Jesus understands. He is with you and can identify with what you're facing. The Good News that

Paul shares is news that we all can relate to. All of us, each and every one, can relate to Jesus!

REFLECTION

1. Do you think Jesus could have been bullied? Why or why not?

2. How does Paul's insights of Jesus change the way you understand Jesus?

3. Have you ever thought about Jesus this way before? Why?

4. What other passages in the Bible seem to support this view of Jesus? What passages challenge this view?

The Under-Dog
Romans 1:3

Okay, one more day and we should have it. The Good News that Paul shares is Great News for all of us. Why? Because sometimes, whether we admit it or not, we feel like failures. And feeling like a failure makes living a victorious Christian life seems completely impossible.

But... What if there was an underdog who shared all my insecurities, social status, and weaknesses? One just like me, who still overcame? What if there was someone who everyone thought would fail, but against all odds, did not fail. What if...

The Jesus that God was so excited to send was not a Jesus that we could not relate to. He did not wear a cape and tights and could not fly. This is Paul's point. Jesus had a human nature. He was a human being, and apparently, an unremarkable one. Everyone relates to this Jesus. Everyone needs this Jesus. He is the Savior of the world. Unlike Superman from Krypton, Jesus came into the world just like everyone else. Jesus overcome, and did so as one of us.

Paul will launch into how Jesus overcame beginning in the next verse and then extending throughout the next eight chapters, will provide the foundation for a call to all mankind to join Him in His overcoming. The point Paul will make begins with a starting point in which all begin — none are super-human and all are equally frail, weak, and helpless.

I don't know about you, but as one who has grown tired of making excuses for un-Christ-like behavior, it is a great encouragement to hear that God has made a way for me to live and overcome, just like Jesus.

REFLECTION

1. In what specific way does this encourage you?

2. In what specific way does this scare you?

3. Some think it's disrespectful to look at Jesus (God who became a man) as a weak, frail, and vulnerable form of humanity? Do you think this is right or wrong? Why?

4. Do you think Jesus was weak, frail and vulnerable? Why or why not?

The Sourced Life
Romans 1:4

"…and who through the Spirit of holiness was declared with power to be the Son of God…"

The Greek word the NIV translates "through" is the preposition κατά. It is a preposition expressing movement, primarily meaning "down" or "down from." In light of this word, a more literal translation of Romans 1:4 could be:

"…and who, down from the Spirit of holiness, was declared with power to be the Son of God…"

…yeah I know, kind of wordy. This is probably why our English word **through** was chosen for the translation. Regardless, the **through** in this verse means **down from**.

Paul's use of κατά is significant and draws the reader's attention to a downward motion of the Spirit. He could have used the preposition διά, also translated **through,** but διά's motion is not downward. Paul seems to want to express a downward movement in relationship to Jesus' connection with the Spirit.

Throughout our Bible, God is understood to be from above and His work in our lives comes from above. In John 3:3, Jesus explains to Nicodemus that he must be born "from above." A few verses later, John describes Jesus as being "from above." (John 3:31) We know that the Spirit came down at Pentecost and during Stephen's stoning, he "looked up" to heaven. (Acts 8:13)

Here's the question... Why all this *above* and *coming down* language when describing Jesus?

REFLECTION

1. Do you think Jesus, as a human being, needed the Spirit? Why or why not?

2. Do you think that just as we are sourced by God, the Spirit also "moved down" upon Jesus? Why or Why not?

3. If Jesus was God, which we know He is, why didn't he just do things out of His own power? Why would he not live out of Himself, but submit to the Spirit's provision? Explain.

The God-Produced Life
Romans 1:4

"…and who through the Spirit of holiness was declared with power to be the Son of God…"

As we found in the last study, the Greek word the NIV translates "through" in our verse is the preposition κατά. It is a preposition expressing movement, primarily meaning "down" or "down from." A more literal translation of Romans 1:4 could be:

"…and who, down from the Spirit of holiness, was declared with power to be the Son of God…"

Paul establishes two things in Romans 1:3-4:

1. Jesus is fully God and fully man. He is not God faking-us-out man, but God embracing-our-fallen-body man.

2. Jesus was moved upon, sourced, by the Holy Spirit.

Around my home church we talk a lot about ***sourcing***. So much so, I often forget that those who don't attend our church may not be familiar with our lingo. Regardless, the concept of ***sourcing*** is easy to understand.

Sourcing = A God-produced life

Christianity is simple. Allow God to produce all that He is through your life. His Thoughts. His Attitudes. His Desires. His Plan. His Purpose. His Motivation. His Power. His Sight. His Understanding. His Love. His Patience. His Forgiveness. His Persistence. His…His…His…

> "…Christ in you, the hope of glory."
> Colossians 1:27

Jesus was the first man since Adam to become the dwelling place of God. The Spirit came down upon Him and remained. In this remarkable man we have been given a glimpse of God's plan for every man.

You were created to be indwelled and possessed by God.

You were created to be inhabited by God.

You were created to sourced.

REFLECTION

1. How could this help you in the struggles you face in your own personal life? Is there any area of your life not sourced by Jesus?

God Produces Holiness
Romans 1:4

"…and who through the Spirit of holiness was declared with power to be the Son of God…"

The Greek word the NIV translates "through" in our verse is the preposition κατά. It is a preposition expressing movement, primarily meaning "down" or "down from." A more literal translation of Romans 1:4 could be:

"…and who, down from the Spirit of holiness, was declared with power to be the Son of God…"

Paul establishes two things in Romans 1:3-4:

1. Jesus is fully God and fully man. He is not God faking-us-out man, but God embracing-our-fallen-body man.

2. Jesus was moved upon by the Holy Spirit. Jesus was sourced by God.

As we have learned, Jesus embraced our helplessness. Jesus embraced man's weakness. Though He was born without sin, Jesus was born in a sin scarred body.

Jesus is just like us, and becoming just like us, demonstrated to us what we're supposed to look like.

Jesus loved the unloveable. Jesus showed mercy to the satanic. Jesus embraced haters. Jesus died for killers. Jesus defeated Satan. Jesus shackled Death. Jesus died to self. Jesus made a way for us to be inhabited by God.

Jesus was led by the Spirit. The Spirit moved down upon Him. "…not as I will, but as You will." (Matthew 26:39)

To be sourced by God is a "not as I will, but as You will" kind of thing.

His Thoughts. His Attitudes. His Desires. His Plan. His Purpose. His Motivation. His Power. His Sight. His Understanding. His Love. His Patience. His Forgiveness. His Persistence. His…His…His…

REFLECTION

1. What would it mean for you to completely surrender your life to Jesus and allow Him to source you?

2. Can you still be a Christian and live for yourself? Is it cool with God for Christians to live selfishly.

Death
Romans 1:4

"...by His resurrection from the dead..."

Death is mankind's enemy, isn't it?

Whenever I think about death, I think about losing my father. I think about the death of my mammy. When I think about facing the possible death of my wife, I inwardly cringe and pray that God would preserve her life. There's no doubting the obvious, I try to avoid death.

Yet I know that death is something that God has allowed into mankind's life. Death surrounds us. Jesus says,

"I tell you the truth, unless a kernel of wheat falls to the ground and dies, it remains only a single seed. But if it dies, it produces many seeds." (John 12:24)

Death is the fabric by which nature renews, sustains, and even preserves itself. Death is apart of life. Death and life are connected.

How can this be? Why would God create such a convoluted and painful system? Why did God create death?

Without death, Adam and Eve would've been sealed by their choice to live independent from God. They would have been cursed … for life. Death was the way out. Death is change. Death is the tragic avenue of mercy in God's plan to save us.

REFLECTION

1. Before we look at resurrection, which is the overcoming of death, we should consider why death is important. For the Christian, death is not the end. For those of us who are united with Christ, death is the beginning.

2. What are your thoughts on death?

3. How does death point us to Jesus?

4. Why do you think God designed life, both physically and in spiritual application, to spring out of death?

Overcoming Death

Romans 1:4

"...by His resurrection from the dead..."

Paul directly links a child of God with overcoming death. Jesus is the Son of God, not just because of His lifestyle, but because His entire life culminated in the event of overcoming the grave. Jesus overcame death.

Death seems to be the path that we all must take. It is the path to resurrection. Just as the seed dies and the new

life-filled sapling springs forth, so also out of death the Life of God springs forth in us.

We are called to death. Unless we take up our cross and DIE, we will never see life. What a strange statement... What an odd suggestion... What does it mean?

We as Christians are called to die to self. We are called to be crucified with Christ. In crucifixion, we live. We no longer live out of our own mindset, our own strength, our own wisdom — our own source. We are called to die to independence from God.

And it is in that death to self, that death to independence from God, we find His Life, His Source, and His Provision. The resurrection is the event where life springs from death.

Jesus declared in John 11:25, "I am the resurrection and the life. He who believes in me will live, even though he dies."

What was Jesus trying to teach Martha? How does believing in Jesus bring life out of death?

When we as Christians embrace Jesus, we find true Life. We continually die to ourselves daily, not living self-sourced, and embrace Him as the source to true Life. God is the fuel, the product, the source by which all of mankind was created to live.

REFLECTION

1. In what area of your life do you desire to no longer live independent from God? In other words, what area of your life do you need to die to yourself?

2. What was the last thing in your life that Jesus called you to die to? Was it difficult?

Through Jesus
Romans 1:5

"Through him and for his name's sake…"

We hear from time to time around the Church people say, "You can do all things through Christ…" Have you ever wondered what that means?

Does it mean that, if I really believe, Jesus can make me fly? That perhaps, if I have enough faith, I won't lose any tennis matches this year? Is the "do all things" about that kind of stuff? If I have enough faith, could I really command mountains to jump into oceans?

Context is everything. You can make any statement mean anything if you change the context. Politicians do this sort of thing all the time. They take something someone says and, after manipulating the context, make that statement convey something it was not supposed to convey. Christians fall victim to this as well. We take Bible passages out of context and they end up meaning something the writer never intended to convey.

Paul writes "Through Him…", in the context of sourcing. It is **through Jesus** or **by Jesus** that we are able to live the life God has called us to live. Living a life sourced by God is the context in which the "through Him…" is written.

REFLECTION

1. I have gotten into the habit of running everything by Jesus. I try to share my thought life with Him, taking every thought captive to His presence. I invite Him into the daily chores and routines of my life. Do you think this is what Paul is suggesting when he writes "Through Him..."?

2. What steps might you begin to take in order to move deeper into a "Through Him..." lifestyle?

3. The Greek word translated **through** in this verse is διά and it suggests a motion through a selected space. We could use it to convey how a boy went **through** the woods on his way home. I wonder what would happen in our daily life if we simply made every decision "Through Him..."?

In Jesus Name
Romans 1:5

"Through him and for his name's sake…"

Have you ever wondered why we end our prayers with "in Jesus name"? Why Jesus told His disciples things like, "You may ask me for anything **in my name** and I will do it." (John 14:14) What's He talking about? What does this mean?

In Bible times, names were important. When someone was assigned a name, especially if it was given by God, that name gave insight into the recipient. Simon was called Peter, the rock, and his name signified his identity in the Church. Jesus' name revealed his character and mission — "…he will save his people from their sins."

To invoke a name is to invoke the identity and purpose of that name into an activity. When I pray "in Jesus name," I am praying in the character and purpose of His name. We do not pray in our own character, with our own intentions. Christians were taught how to pray. Prayer is the alignment of our heart with the heart of Jesus.

As Paul moves into the next few verses, elaborating on our calling and mission as the body of Christ, he firmly insists that calling and mission is **through** Jesus and **for His name's sake**.

Simply put, the Church is nothing short of the extension of Jesus Himself.

REFLECTION

1. There are two things that jump out at me in light of this verse. First, why do we compartmentalize our day into spiritual and unspiritual? I mean, I invoke Jesus' name into my 3-squares-a-day meal times, asking for His blessing over my food. If I'm really spiritual, I may begin and end my day with Him, praying when I get up and before I go to bed.

2. I wonder . . . Should I compartmentalized my day? Shouldn't I drive my car "for His name's sake" just like I eat my meals? What would His presence would change in your life If this happened?

3. Second, I feel that I personally have been guilty of cheapening the "in the name of Jesus" stuff in my own life. I mean, am I really eating the food He would eat? Am I honoring Him by my food choice or just tacking on a spiritual prayer before the routine of eating? How do you feel?

Grace
Romans 1:5

"Through him and for his name's sake, we received **grace...**"

Operating out of the provision of the Holy Spirit, living a life sourced by God, translates into receiving grace. We who experience life "Through Him," seeing as He sees and feeling as He feels, and live "for His name's sake," live with His purpose, receive from Him what is essential for the mission of the Kingdom. We receive grace.

Without grace, the mission of the Kingdom through the Church would fail. It is by grace we are saved and by that same grace we live a life fruitful and productive in the Kingdom. We are measured not by performance, but by grace. God judges us not by the outcome, but in grace, judges us on whether or not we have lived "Through Him" and "for His name's sake."

Notice how and where Paul places **grace** in his statement. Grace follows both **through** and **for His name's sake**. These two lifestyle character traits are the avenue of grace. When we lived sourced by God, all that we say and do are covered by His grace. Just as the child who sloppily paints a picture for his daddy and receives the praise of having that master piece displayed on his daddy's desk, so also God takes the Christian's inadequate act of love and receives it with joy. Both the child and the Christian receive grace, not because of their skill or talent, but because of His grace.

REFLECTION

1. Motive and intent are most important to God. What are your motives on how you live? Do you obey God out of fear or obligation?

2. Where do you sometimes live for God with wrong motives?

3. How does it make you feel to know that God desires a love relationship with you and not just for you to obey Him?

4. How does Paul's statement change the way you describe Christianity to unbelievers?

Cheapening Grace
Romans 1:5

"Through him and for his name's sake, we received **grace**…"

From my observations, I would say that among all the terms in the Bible, **grace** has been misused and misinterpreted the most.

God's grace seems to be commonly used as an excuse to live in ungodly ways. From the sexually immoral to those who lie, grace is used as a catch-word for "hey, no body's perfect." Statements like "I now this is not what God wants me to do, but He understands. His grace covers this," reveal an inconsistency with how Paul describes grace.

Grace is the fruit of "for His name's sake." God gives grace to those who love Him and seek to live in a way that honors Him. Those who receive grace live in a love relationship with Jesus Christ. They are not judged by God for mistakes made, but because their motives are noble and right, they are forgiven even before they ask. Judgement is on motive, not outcome.

REFLECTION

1. Religious people seem to be obsessed with rules.

What does this passage teach us about the kind of relationship God wants to have with us?

2. Do you know of anyone who uses grace as excuse to live in a way that displeases Jesus? If so, what do you think your responsibility as a Christian is to that person?

3. How could this passage help you talk with people about Jesus?

Apostleship
Romans 1:5

"Through him and for his name's sake, we received grace and *apostleship*..."

If you've spent anytime around church, you might have heard of the 12 Apostles. Formerly disciples, the apostles were those who were chosen by Jesus to be His witnesses. They were chosen, called, and sent as Apostles into the world to bear witness to the Gospel of Jesus Christ.

The word *apostle* is a translation of the word apostolés, the feminine form of the noun apostéllō. This word means "to dispatch" or "to send forth."

What is interesting about apostleship, is how it can be unique and yet not so unique. The 12 Apostles were unique, because they were the first to be sent. However, as Paul informs us in our passage, though they were the first to be sent, they were not to be the only ones sent.

"Through him and for his name's sake, we received grace and *apostleship*..."

Every Christian is called to the mission of the Kingdom. We are all called to be apostles.

REFLECTION

1. Do you view yourself as a missionary? Why or why not?

2. Every missionary has a mission field. If you are a Christian, you are a missionary. Could your mission field be your home? Your school? Your workplace?

3. Is it possible to be a Christian and yet reject the mission of apostleship?

Sourced to Obey
Romans 1:5

"...to the obedience that comes through faith..."

It is evident, not only from Paul's letter to the Romans, but also throughout the NT, that all Christians are called to share the Gospel with the world. We are all called to be missionaries.

What is our message? What is the specific call we are to give to those in whom we share Jesus?

Paul tells us we are to share about an obedience that comes only through faith. The message of the Gospel is not just to obey, to just do whatever God tells us to do. We are called to have faith, a faith that produces obedience.

Once again, Paul returns to the subject of living a life empowered by God. We are called to live out of His strength, not trusting to our own. The Christian life is all about faith, about living a life empowered by His presence. Then and only then, being empowered by His strength, can we live obediently before Him.

REFLECTION

1. Do you think it is easy to fall into the trap of "rule keeping" when living our life for Jesus? Why or why not?

2. Is it possible to live a life pleasing to God out of our own strength and insight? How does Jesus make a difference in your own obedience?

3. Do you have an area of your life where you are not obedient to Jesus? If so, could it be that area of your life is absent of the presence of Jesus?

I am His
Romans 1:6

"…called to belong to Jesus Christ."

It doesn't take long, after we've come to "follow Jesus," that we realize God wants more than service and devotion to Him.

God wants us.

The Greek word we translate "belong" means just what you think it means. When a person accepts Jesus into their life, they become the property of God. They belong to Jesus.

God doesn't want servants, nor slaves. God wants children. God's design for mankind reaches beyond servants who obey Him. He created you and I to be His very own. Similar to the way I look at my son or daughter, God looks upon me. I am His and He is mine. Our intimacy is extreme, our relationship is family.

The enemy wants to convince us that we are alone, that even though God loves us, He is far away. At best looking down upon us from the Heavens, His love and presence is far away. This, of course, is not consistent with how Paul describes God's desire for us. We belong to Him. He is alway with us. To belong to God is to be His cherished possession, His dearest child whom He never leaves alone.

Sometimes life is harder than normal. Sometimes we feel all alone. Whether its financial hardship or persecution or sadness or loneliness or…Whatever we face, He is present with us.

REFLECTION

1. Have you ever felt alone? How does Paul's encouragement to the church in Rome encourage you?

2. How might realizing God's presence change the way you face trouble at school or work?

3. Would you be willing to give your attention to Jesus throughout your week this week? Every moment, realize He's present with you? You belong to Him! Don't despair, don't give up hope, He is with you and has a plan for you in whatever you are facing.

Loved as Saints
Romans 1:7

"To all in Rome who are loved by God and called to be saints…"

I remember studying the saints in college. Depicted on stained-glass-windows, they seemed so lofty and benevolent. Most looked like monks to me, men who dedicated their life to solitude and study. They never married, had no children, and lived their lives removed from society in service of the Church. They are the saints, so different than myself.

Yet this seems so different than Paul's language in this passage. He calls all Christians saints, from the least to the greatest among us. All who profess Christ, none are excluded.

Is this right? Is this who I am in Jesus? A saint…really?

Scholars tell us the fundamental idea behind the word **saint** does not necessarily suggest Christianity. That is to say, the word saint is not always applied to those who are filled with the Holy Spirit. Like my mom used to say, whenever someone did something she liked; "you are a saint!"

The term saint can be understood as — "Its fundamental idea is separation, consecration, devotion to the service of Deity, sharing in God's purity and abstaining from earth's defilement."

It makes me wonder... Does that really describe me? I am fundamentally His? Am I separated from all things apposed to Him and consecrated to Him alone? Am I devoted to His purpose and character? Is my relationship with Him so precious, so intimate, that I abstain from the lusts and longings of this world. Am I His? Am I a saint?

REFLECTION

1. You are not second class. You are not less-than. You are invited into intimacy with Jesus, called by Him to sainthood. Are you responding to that call?

2. What area of your life might be conflicting with the call of sainthood?

3. Do you think saint is an **option** among many who profess to be Christian. Is sainthood the only option?

4. Is Christianity an all or nothing thing? Can you just partially belong to Jesus? Explain...

Peace
Romans 1:7

"...grace and **peace** to you..."

There are certain words that I call "old fashioned." What I mean is, there are words that we either don't use anymore or whose meaning have changed. Asunder, bane, and mooncalf are examples of outdated words, while gay and flirt have changed their meaning. I can't do it here, but you should look them up, its kinda funny.

I think **peace** is one of these "old fashioned" words. Whether that means we don't use it much anymore or that we understand it in a new way, **peace** has lost some meaning. At least, from a Christian perspective.

Paul tells the church in Rome that peace comes from God the Father and the Lord Jesus Christ. Being reconciled with God, walking in intimacy with Jesus, is what brings peace.

I don't think the young can fully recognize how important peace is. I know I didn't, not during my teens, nor in my 20's. In my 30's, I become much more aware of my need for peace. I needed rest, security, and the knowledge that everything was going to be alright. This becomes more pronounced the older I get. Why? Because I am away from mom and dad, the security blanket is gone. It's just me, my wife, and my children. I have a family, property, an aging body, and retirement to think about. It can be a lot of pressure.

Yet as Christian, I live in the REALITY that I am not the maker of my own destiny. Jesus is blazing a trail before me, leading me and sustaining me to a future He desires. I trust Him. In Him, I have peace.

REFLECTION

1. Do you or anyone you know suffer from depression or anxiety? What's that like?

2. Can a person have peace and be depressed at the same time? Why or why not?

3. How can the peace of Jesus Christ cure non-clinical depression? How might Jesus be the cure for living anxious and depressed?

4. Do you think there might be a connection between all types of depression and spirituality? Why?

Light in the Darkness
Romans 1:8

"…reported all over the world."

Paul's opening statement to the Church in Rome about their faith and how it is world renown reminds me of what I've seen in my own lifetime. Whether the revival in Asbury or the movement of God in Florida a few years ago, when God moves in a body of believers, the world takes notice.

We are called to be a light in the darkness, salt to a famished world, and a voice of hope to the hopeless. These are not exceptional characteristics of the Church, they are supposed to be the norm. Like the church in Rome, we too are to possess a faith in Jesus that gains the attention of all who touch our lives.

I travel and preach. I am blessed, extraordinarily so, to be used by Jesus in the lives of those who are seeking Truth. I receive both criticism and compliments, the latter more often thankfully. Yet the greatest complement I've ever received come indirectly from my son during a conversation with one of his friends.

They were talking about using fowl language, curse words and vulgarity. The conversation was not organized and typical with junior high kids, a bit chaotic. Yet in the midst of asking each other if they used this kind of language, one asked CJ if he'd ever heard me "cuss." In CJ's typical flamboyant way, he responded animatedly with "NO! He loves Jesus."

Although I desire the world to see God in my life, I am thankful that my children see clearly my relationship with Jesus Christ. He is a priority over all things to me and they see it plainly. Praise the Lord!

REFLECTION

1. How loudly does your life speak Jesus?

2. We have touched on already our call to the mission field. We are all missionaries to our own context of life. How does this passage challenge you in your own mission field?

3. How do you witness to a lost world without being judgmental or offensive?

The Heart Level
Romans 1:9

"God, whom I serve with my whole heart…"

Christianity is concerned with the matters of the heart. From just a quick read through the 27 letters in our NT, one becomes overwhelmed with the magnitude of emphasis on heart change.

Far to often, Christianity is shoved into the realm of activities. Christians are supposed to do **this** or to not do **that**. From church attendance to money given, people often evaluate themselves by their activities, or the lack there of, that make up their daily life.

This kind of approach, not only in any relationship, but certainly with Jesus Christ, completely disregards the focus of the Gospel message as proposed in the Bible. Relationship always moves beyond activities into matters of the heart.

I learned this early on in my marriage. The gifts and "little things" I did for my wife were recognized as acts of love. This is what made them more than activities to her. This is what she wanted.

Our relationship with God is the same. Paul will expound on this throughout his book, but in chapter 12 he will really bring it home. He writes,

"Therefore, I urge you, brothers, in view of God's mercy, to offer your bodies as living sacrifices, holy and pleasing to God—this is your spiritual act of worship." (Romans 12:1)

True worship is not merely sacrifice, but a daily living our lives to please God. Worship is more than activities, more than routine acts of service.

REFLECTION

1. We all are subject to routines. From praying before meals to tucking our children into bed, routines make up our daily lives. How might the spiritual routines of our day take on more of a Romans 12:1 emphasis?

2. Paul stresses that living a life pleasing to God reaches beyond religious activities. Do you think this makes certain Christian disciplines, like morning devotions and person prayer times, less significant? Why or why not?

Preachers
Romans 1:9

"…in preaching the gospel of his Son…"

I am a preacher. So, whenever I read verses like this one, they resonate with me on a level I understand. I know what it is to stand and share the Word before a congregation. I know what it feels like, I can identify with Paul.

But what about those who do not stand before congregations? What about those who do not preach? How do they receive this verse?

Many years ago, while preaching and teaching with Dr. Stephen Manley in South Africa, I witnessed a young girl performing a dance during a service. It was in the place of where we Americans would expect to find a special song or instrumental. In the middle of her routine, Stephen leaned over to me and said, "**that** is preaching!"

His worlds moved me. He saw something special in her performance. What he saw was beyond the moves and beyond the music. She was expressing the message of the song, which happened to be about Jesus, through the eloquence of dance.

I catalogued that event in my mind that day, for it spoke to my heart about preaching. As I think back on that moment, all those years ago, I wonder to myself; aren't we all, in our own special way, preachers of the Gospel of Jesus Christ? Aren't we all proclaimers of the Good News?

Isn't the teacher in the classroom, the mechanic in his shop, the engineer on his computer, and the doctor in his operating room, all performers on a stage? There may be no music and there may be no written prose, but regardless of the vehicle, the message is the same and an audience is listening. We are indeed all preachers in our own way.

REFLECTION

1. Do you know where God is calling you to service? Where do you think your pulpit will be 10 years from now?

2. Where is your pulpit currently?

3. Do you view yourself as currently having a pulpit? Do you see yourself as a preacher? Why or why not?

Spiritual Gifts
Romans 1:9-11

"...that I may impart to you some spiritual gift..."

If you've spent any time around the Church, you might have heard of spiritual gifts. In our verse, Paul has been praying eagerly for the church in Rome, and specifically that he might come and "impart" to them some spiritual gift.

When Paul says "impart," he is writing about teaching those in Rome about who they are in Christ. Every member of the body of Christ is gifted for the edification of that body and for the work of the Kingdom. Everyone has gifts to share.

I have often described my calling as nothing more than reminding the body of who they are in Christ. This is necessary, for I think we tend to forget or we get distracted from who we are. I also think we have a tendency to deem our presence in the Church as dispensable or insignificant. This is completely false and, from time to time, we need reminded of who we are in Jesus and how significant we are to Kingdom ministry.

Thus, Paul calls each to embrace his own gift, participating in the ministry God has prepared each to serve. Whether that be in the gift of healing or that of prophecy, all have been called to labor.

Gifts of the Spirit are bestowed upon mankind by selection, but as Paul teaches elsewhere, each gift is bestowed in its proper place. God desires to spill through each person in the body of Christ in a unique way, according to their ordained gifting. In other words, God has designed each of us for His set purpose, each to his or her own work.

REFLECTION

1. Do you know where God has called you to service in His body? If not, how might you discover your gift? If so, how are you participating in the ministry of the Kingdom?

2. Is it possible that there are some who have no gifting in the body? Why or why not?

3. Is it possible to be a Christian and yet not participate in Kingdom work? Can you be a Christian and not be used by Jesus? Why or why not?

Encouraged
Romans 1:12

"…that you and I may be mutually encouraged by each other's faith."

Encouragement takes many forms. I am a basketball fan and I like to watch the NBA. My favorite team is the Golden State Warriors. There is much I could write about the Warriors, from their amazing talent to the flow of their offense. They are just a fun team to watch. Yet one of the things I like most about their team is the level of encouragement they give one another. Whether in response to a deep three or a crazy no-look pass, those on the bench seem always to be the biggest and most outrageous fans in the building.

When I read in the NT about the body of Christ, how they are to labor together and spur one another along in the faith, I think of the Warrior's bench. I believe we are called to such enthusiasm. We are called to give such encouragement.

In Luke 15:10, Jesus speaks of the Heavenly Host with such enthusiastic language. He says,

"In the same way, I tell you, there is rejoicing in the presence of the angels of God over one sinner who repents."

Notice it is not the angels, but those in the presence of the angels who are rejoicing! It makes me wonder...Are we on the **court** of Kingdom ministry, and if so, are those who've gone before us on the **bench** in Heaven cheering us on? I can almost hear them cheering as I write!

REFLECTION

1. Do you ever need encouragement in your Christian journey? When was the last time you received encouragement and how did it help you?

2. Do you know of anyone who needs encouragement? How might you cheer them on in their current situation?

3. How might we use social media as avenues of encouragement?

Power
Romans 1:16

"I am not ashamed of the gospel, because it is the power of God for the salvation of everyone who believes: first for the Jew, then for the Gentile."

There are many passages in our Bible in which have become, for the lack of a better phrase, **bumper-sticker** quotes. Paul's testimony in this verse is one of those passages. Like other well known passages, Romans 1:16 seems to sum up all that Christians believe and need to continually hear concerning the Good News of Jesus Christ.

I have several passages written down in the front of my Bible. Some are for guidance in prayer, some are for encouragement in times of struggle, and some are simple reminders of who I am in Christ. Romans 1:16 is among those in the cover of my Bible and it has often served as a reminder of not only who I am in Christ, but the power of God that is available to me in times of struggle and temptation.

But what does Paul mean by "…the power of God for salvation?" What **power** does he speak of? Is it the power to huff and puff and blow the enemy's house down? Is it the power to leap tall buildings in a single bound? What does the Gospel empower me to do or overcome?

There are many reference to power in the NT, but here in this verse, Paul speaks of the power of salvation. When we accept the message of the Gospel, that Jesus came to reconcile us back to God, the Holy Spirit comes and indwells the newly-made Christian. We are a new creation. We are not our old self, but are a combination of all that we are and all that He is. We are different due to His presence within us.

…and when God indwells a person, when they are "saved," that person is filled with the power that is inherent to God alone.

Throughout the Bible, we constantly hear of the power of God and how it surpasses the power of man. Mankind was created to live, not out of their own power, but in the power of God. It is His fruit that displays itself in our life. It is His power that enables us to break free from the enemy. When we receive the Holy Spirit, we receive all the power of God to live a life free from every bondage and trap this world can present. We have access to His power. We can live free!

REFLECTION

1. Have you ever experienced the power of God in your personal life? Explain?

2. Would you call resisting the devil's temptations the power of God? Why or why not?

3. Ability is a kind of power. Given the ability to understand Scripture is a result of the power of God. God grants understanding, God grants revelation. Have you ever experienced revelation like this?

4. I witnessed my son's healing when he was 2 years old. God's power worked through a man who prayed for my son. Have you ever witnessed a healing?

5. Do you think Christians sometimes doubt God's power in their life? That, perhaps, God cannot heal them or help them overcome something their facing? Why do you think people struggle with unbelief?

Made in the USA
Columbia, SC
20 June 2018